# DOLPHINS!

*White-sided dolphins and a Pacific black whale perform at Sea World. Opposite page: Bottle-nosed dolphin*

# DOLPHINS!

## by June Behrens

CHILDRENS PRESS ®

CHICAGO

Dedicated to John Olguin for his lifelong service to children

*The author wishes to acknowledge with thanks the assistance of John Olguin, Director Emeritus, Cabrillo Marine Museum, San Pedro, California, and Bill Samaras of the American Cetacean Society*

**PHOTO CREDITS**
Art Resource—7 (both photos), 41
Earthviews:
  © Kenneth C. Balcomb III—9
  © Randall S. Wells—10
  © Robert Pitman—17, 27
  © P. Arnantho—18
  © Marc Webber—23
  © Stephen Leatherwood—28
  © Jeff Jacobson—29
  © Ted Stephenson—30
  © Stan Minasian—31
Institute of Hydrobiology—32
Marineworld/Africa USA:
  © Darryl W. Bush—36, 38, 39
  © Phillip Rosenberg—24, 25
  © Sea World—2, 6, 13, 21, 40, back cover
  (bottom)

Tom Stack and Associates:
  © Ed Robinson—1
  © Brian Parker—Front cover, 11, 20, 22, 45
  © Jeff Foot—33, back cover (top)
Valan Photos:
  © Stephen Krasemann—3
  © Jeff Foot—8, 14, 19
  © Kennon Cooke—15
  © Richard Sears—16
  © J. A. Wilkinson—23
  © R. C. Simpson—35
Karen Yops—5, 37
Cover: Atlantic bottle-nosed dolphin
Back cover: Bottle-nosed dolphin (top)
                Commerson's dolphin (bottom)

**Library of Congress Cataloging-in-Publication Data**

Behrens, June.
  Dolphins! / by June Behrens.
    p.    cm.
  Includes index.
  Summary: Describes the appearance, reproduction, infancy, social behavior, and intelligence of this remarkable sea mammal.
  ISBN 0-516-00517-0
  1. Dolphins—Juvenile literature.
  [1. Dolphins.] I. Title.
QL737.C432B45    1989                    89-33846
599.5′3—dc20                                 CIP
                                                    AC

*A trainer and dolphin do a trick that is bound to be a crowd-pleaser.*

# Contents

*Common dolphin with Pacific black whales*

## What Is a Dolphin?

A sleek body leaps high out of the water. It turns in the air and splashes into the sea. Up from a deep dive, the animal races through the water at 25 miles an hour. This truly remarkable animal is a dolphin. It has been admired and respected by people through the ages.

*Dolphins are pictured on this fifteenth century pitcher (left) and on the walls of a building in Knossos on the island of Crete.*

From earliest times humans and dolphins have been friends. Ancient Greek stories tell of this friendship. Pictures and coins of long ago show people riding dolphins. Dolphins have saved human lives. They have often befriended people. They have guided ships to safety.

*Killer whale swimming off Vancouver Island*

Dolphins are mammals, just as humans are. They breathe air and the babies drink their mother's milk. Dolphins are warm-blooded and have backbones. They are members of the cetacean group of mammals. Their cousins are whales and porpoises. Scientists tell us that cetaceans are mammals that went to live in the sea millions of years ago.

A dolphin breathes through its blowhole—

a nostril, or opening for breathing—on top of its head. Dolphins blow out used air and draw fresh air into their lungs through the blowholes. They can close the blowholes and stay underwater for up to six minutes. When dolphins sleep, they take little naps near the water surface. They bob up and down, coming to the surface to breathe.

*Porpoises are related to dolphins and whales.*

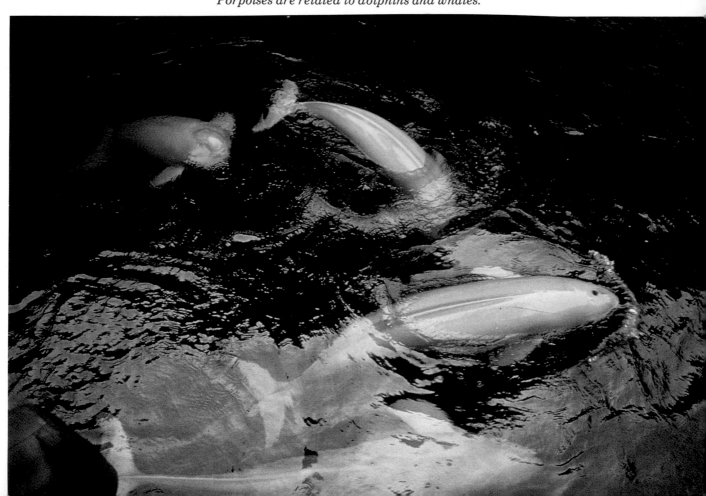

*Spinner dolphins*

*Bottle-nosed dolphin with its trainer*

The dolphin's flat, horizontal tail is called a fluke. Flippers are the paddles dolphins use for swimming. The powerful fluke and flippers help to make the dolphin one of the fastest swimmers in the sea. The bones of the flipper and of the human hand are very much alike.

11

Most dolphins have dark colors on the upper body and lighter colors on the underside. This coloring helps protect dolphins from their enemies. Several members of the dolphin family have striking black and white markings.

Dolphins are noisy animals. They chirp and whistle and squeak. They make these sounds by shifting air between the nasal sacs inside their skull. We can make dolphin-like sounds when we let air out of a balloon. Dolphins also

*Pacific dolphins*

*Scientists record and study dolphin sounds.*

make sounds by slapping their flukes and flippers on the water. They clap their jaws together and make noisy splashes. People think these action sounds express dolphins' feelings.

Dolphins use sound to help them see. When a dolphin "talks," the sound travels through the water. When the sound hits an object, it bounces back toward the dolphin. The echo

*Dr. John Ford is conducting an acoustic study of killer whales.*

the dolphin hears tells it that solid things are near. Scientists call this echolocation, or sonar.

Dolphins are sometimes called small, toothed whales. They have more teeth than any other animal. Some members of the family have over two hundred. Scientists can tell the age of a dolphin by the rings on its teeth. Dolphins live for about twenty-five years.

*Dolphins are sometimes called small, toothed whales.*

*A herd, or pod, of common dolphins*

## Dolphin Herds

Dolphins live in the oceans of the world. They travel in herds. Smaller groups, known as pods, are a part of the large herds. Dolphins work and play together. They take care of one another.

When a member of the pod is in trouble, other dolphins are there to help. Two dolphins will swim on each side of a sick animal. They will help the animal to the surface to breathe. Female dolphins care for a baby while its mother swims away to find food.

Dolphin groups often work as a team in finding their food. They take turns and share in the feeding. Dolphins need their friends and companions. They are not happy when separated from their herd. If left alone, some scientists believe that wild dolphins might die of loneliness.

*Pacific spinner dolphins*

*Irrawaddy dolphins*

## Baby Dolphins

The mother dolphin has one baby. When it
is time for the baby to be born, other dolphins
gather around to protect the mother from
danger. After the birth, the mother pushes her
baby to the surface of the water. The baby
must breathe air at once. The mother has a
female dolphin friend who helps with the
baby.

The baby looks just like its mother, only smaller. It "talks" to its mother in squeaks and whistles. The mother nurses her baby, just as other mammal mothers do. The mother dolphin squirts milk into the baby's mouth from the two teats on the underside of her body.

The baby drinks mother's milk for as long as eighteen months. It stays close to its mother's side. The mother is its teacher and protector.

*Killer whale with her calf*

## Members of the Family

There are more than thirty kinds of dolphins. They belong to the family Delphinidae.

The *bottle-nosed dolphin* gets its name from the shape of its beak, a mouth part of the dolphin. The bottle-nosed dolphin grows to a length of twelve feet. An adult might weigh over 400 pounds. This dolphin feeds on many kinds of fish. The bottle-nosed dolphin swims in all the oceans except those in the colder polar regions. It is easily trained in captivity and is often seen performing in marine parks.

*Atlantic bottle-nosed dolphins (opposite page and below) are easily trained.*

*Pacific white-sided dolphin*

The *Pacific white-sided dolphin* swims in North Pacific waters. It has a short beak and a hooked, pointed dorsal fin on its back. The Pacific white-sided dolphin has two stripes running from its head to near its tail. This dolphin often travels with other members of the family, including the right-whale dolphin and pilot whales.

*Risso's dolphin* swims in warm and tropical waters. It is usually light gray with dark or black flippers, dorsal fin, and fluke. Its rounded forehead, called the melon, has a crease down the middle. The Risso's dolphin does not have a beak. This dolphin lives in herds of twenty or more.

*Risso's dolphin*

*Spinner dolphin in flight*

The *spinner dolphin* can leap from the water and spin its body two times in the air. Its long, slender body reaches a length of over six feet. There are short-snouted and long-snouted spinners. They might travel in herds of over 1,000. Spinners are deep-water dolphins, found in the warmer tropical oceans.

The *spotted dolphin* is named for its unusual coloring. It gets more spots as it grows older. The spotted dolphin has a long beak and a tall dorsal fin on its back. With the seasons, the herd might move from inshore to offshore in tropical and warmer oceans.

*Pod of spotted dolphins*

*Common dolphin leaps from the water.*

The *common dolphin* has a slender body and a long beak. The upper body is dark in color, with a light to white belly. The common dolphin travels in large, noisy herds. Common dolphins often hitch rides on waves made by passing ships. Members of this family are often called the acrobats of the sea.

The *southern right-whale dolphin* has no dorsal fin. Its coloring is black and white. Herds have been seen in temperate coastal waters as well as in deep ocean waters to the south. The *northern right-whale dolphin* is found in the temperate North Pacific Ocean. It has no dorsal fin and its coloring is mostly black.

*Northern right-whale dolphins*

*Commerson's dolphins*

*Commerson's dolphin* lives in colder waters of the southern oceans. It has a thick, stocky body and no beak. It has an unusual black and white pattern in its coloring, and the dorsal fin is rounded past the middle of the back. The Commerson's dolphin usually travels in small pods of ten or twelve.

The *killer whale*, or *orca*, is the largest member of the dolphin family. It swims in all the oceans. A male might grow to thirty feet and weigh more than eight tons. The black and white coloring and the giant dorsal fin help to identify the killer whale. Herds of up to thirty members roam the seas and attack whales, birds, seals, squid, and many kinds of fish.

*The mighty killer whale is the largest member of the dolphin family.*

*Ganges River dolphin or Ganges susu*

# River Dolphins

Some dolphins live in the rivers of the world. Their family name is Platanistidae.

The *Ganges susu* is found in the Ganges River in India. Its eyes are the size of pinholes and the dorsal fin is a tiny hump. This "blind" river dolphin has a long, narrow beak. It is often found alone or in pairs. It might grow to a length of eight feet or more.

The *boutu* lives in the Amazon and Orinoco river basins of South America. This dolphin grows to ten feet. It uses its long beak to find fish on the muddy river bottom. It has a thick body and broad flippers. Boutus are very slow-moving dolphins.

*Amazon River dolphin or boutu*

The *beiji* swims in the Yangtze River in China. This dolphin is built like the other river dolphins. Coloring is pale gray and whitish on the underside. Little is known about this rare dolphin.

*River dolphin or beiji*

## Are Dolphins Smart?

The dolphin brain is about the size of a human brain. The layer of gray matter over most of the brain is called the cortex. Cetaceans and humans have the best-developed cortex structures in the animal kingdom.

Dolphins think ahead and plan. They learn and remember tricks. They can make up their

own games and they can solve problems. All these activities show intelligence.

Trainers at oceanariums know how quickly dolphins learn. Many dolphins love to entertain. They like being "stars" and doing their tricks. Young dolphins love to learn for the fun of it, not for the reward.

Dolphins make up hunting and chasing games. They tease and play tricks on other sea animals and humans. They teach other dolphins their throw-and-catch and chase games. Dolphins have been taught lifesaving by their trainers.

*Atlantic bottle-nosed dolphin*

*Jim Mullen works with a dolphin.*

At Marineworld/Africa USA in California, trainer Jim Mullen taught his dolphins to clean out their tank when trash blew in. They were rewarded with a fish for each bit of paper or trash. One dolphin brought Jim far more trash than the others, and he wondered why. He checked the bottom of the tank and found that this dolphin had a collection of trash under the platform. The dolphin would tear a small piece from its collection (or savings) and take it to Jim for the reward. This dolphin was thinking and planning ahead.

## Dolphins Go to School

Kae, a bottle-nosed dolphin in Hawaii, plays a game of twenty questions with biologist Earl Murchison. She nudges a red ball to answer the questions with yes. Nudging the blue ball is a no answer. Scientist Murchison and Kae are communicating with each other.

At Flipper Sea School in Florida, dolphins learn to choose and give right answers to trainers' questions.

Dr. Diana Reiss at Marineworld/Africa USA in California works with two young male dolphins and their mothers. She is learning how Pan and Delphi talk to each other and to their mothers.

Dr. Reiss is the teacher and Pan and Delphi are her students. She swims with her students and they are good friends. When the dolphins want something, they must ask for it. There are three push buttons in the pool. When Pan and Delphi push the right button, they get what they want.

If a dolphin wants a ball, it nudges the triangle button. If it pushes the H button, it will get a hug or a pat. A press of the notched figure on the third button will bring the dolphin a plastic ring to play with.

Each time the dolphin pushes one of the buttons, a computer makes a special whistling

*Dr. Diana Reiss sets up experiments (left and opposite page) that test the learning ability of her dolphins.*

sound for that button. The dolphins sometimes make that sound before they push one of the buttons. When they get their ball, they will imitate the sound for ball. They are talking "dolphinese."

Training schools in Hawaii, Florida, and California have helped us to know more about dolphins. Scientists tell us there is much more to learn from and about these intelligent animals.

*The image of a boy on a dolphin appears in the art of many different countries.*

## Dolphins and Humans

Two thousand years ago, Plutarch of Chaeronea, a famous Greek philosopher, wrote "To the dolphin alone, beyond all others, nature has granted what the best philosophers seek: friendship for no advantage. Though it has no need at all of any man, yet it is a genial friend to all and has helped many."

Hundreds of stories have been told about dolphins and humans. These friendly, social mammals often seek human companionship. They seem able to sense danger. At sea, they have helped people in distress, just as they help members of their herd in trouble. Here are just a few of the many stories about the dolphins.

In 1978 a small fishing boat off the coast of South Africa was trapped in a dense fog. The fishermen claimed four dolphins saved their lives. For an hour and a half, the dolphins nudged the boat through dangerous waters, guiding it to the shore and safety.

As long as they can remember, the Imragen tribe in coastal northwest Africa have given the dolphin a godlike reverence. They depend on their catch of mullet fish for survival. From the beach, tribal members sight schools of mullet. They beat the water with sticks as a signal, calling the dolphins for help. Faithful dolphins go to work herding the mullet into the nets of the Imragens.

A newspaper story reported the life-saving measures of three dolphins. When a yacht exploded, a woman was thrown bleeding and injured into the water. The dolphins swam to her and took positions to keep her afloat. The dolphins stayed with her until she was able to climb onto a floating buoy and wait for rescuers to come.

There are many documented cases of dolphins saving humans in trouble. Drowning swimmers have been shoved toward shallow water. Ships have been guided and seamen have been rescued.

One of the most famous dolphins of all was Pelorus Jack. From 1888 to the 1920s this Risso's dolphin guided and followed ships through Cook Strait in New Zealand. People from around the world came to New Zealand to see Pelorus Jack.

Dolphins have sought out humans for companionship. Opo, a bottle-nosed dolphin, visited regularly and gave rides to the children at Opononi Beach in New Zealand. For a year, the children played ball and other games with Opo.

Nina, another bottle-nosed dolphin, became friends with the people at Lorbe Cove near La Corogna, Spain. She even rescued a swimmer. Grateful friends erected a monument in Nina's honor.

At Dolphins Plus in Key Largo, Florida, people can swim with the dolphins. The Borguss family and other teachers tell visitors about dolphins and how humans must protect them.

Before people swim with the dolphins, they must go to "school" for an hour. Trainers tell them what to expect and how dolphins behave. Then the people may swim with the dolphins for about half an hour. The dolphins decide

how long they want to swim with the people.

Dolphins swim in a canal at Dolphins Plus that is open to the sea. They can swim out and into the ocean at any time. But the dolphins stay at Dolphins Plus. They have the love and friendship of their trainers. They have enough food to eat and they are protected from their enemies. And, they are entertained by their visitors!

# Glossary

**acrobat** (AK • roh • bat) — a performer who is skilled in such feats as tumbling and tightrope walking

**blowhole** (BLOH • hole) — the opening for breathing on the top of the head of whales and dolphins

**cetacean** (sih • TAY • shun) — one of a group of mammals that live in water

**cortex** (KOR • tex) — a layer of gray matter on the surface of the brain

**Delphinidae** (del • FIN • ih • day) — the family of cetaceans to which many dolphins belong

**dolphin** (DOLL • fin) — a mammal that lives in water and looks like a small whale

**dorsal** (DOR • sil) — on or near the back

**echolocation** (ek • oh • loh • KAY • shun) — a means of finding objects by sending out sounds and receiving the echoes that bounce back

**flipper** (FLIH • per) — a broad, flat limb used for swimming

**fluke** (FLOOK) — the broad, flat tail of a dolphin, used for swimming

**gray matter** (GRAY MAT • er) — grayish tissue in the brain that contains nerves

**herd** (HERD) — a large group of animals that travel together

**horizontal** (hor • ih ZAHN • til) — level, flat

**inshore** (in • SHOHR) — in the ocean water near the shore

**mammal** (MAM • il) — one of a group of warm-blooded animals that have hair and nurse their young with milk

46